Group Activities For Kids Who Hurt

Providing Help Through Loss and Transition

Sally Jo Blair

ISBN - 10: 1-56499-077-8

ISBN - 13: 978-1-56499-077-8

INNERCHOICE Publishing
15079 Oak Chase Court
Wellington, FL 33414

www.InnerchoicePublishing.com

Dedicated to Free

Acknowledgments

My gratitude overflows to so many wonderful folks who, as my teachers and friends, seek the very best in me. To Bob, my loving husband who believes I can do anything I set my mind to do. And Josh, my son, who encourages me to set my mind to anything I believe I can't do. To Annie, who, through many devoted years of teaching, has continued to hold the vision of each and every child as special and capable. To Mary Linda, whose joy I treasure. To Mary, whose courage astounds me. To Susanna, who believed there was this book in me, and helped me to birth it. And to Billy and Pegge Lynn, who inspire me daily on the value of love, service and living my truth.

Preface

As a small child, I received the gift of a single yellow rosebud. Longing for its fragrance and impatient to see it in full bloom, I forced it open petal by petal. I recall the grief I felt when I no longer held a rose, but a collection of bruised petals.

During my many years of working with children in groups, I've often been reminded of that rose. Collectively we gather to form a bouquet, each bearing our own set of concerns, strengths and vulnerabilities. Some come on like gangbusters, ready to confront, rebel against the pain, tear up the rose and move on. Others come thorny, perhaps not even aware of the potential to bloom beyond the sharps. Still others are fragile, withdrawing into their roots, needing the safety of silence. Others arrive ready to bloom, yet in need of a safe place to take that risk. Handled with care, we can each blossom intact. Unlike my yellow rose, we do not have to be torn, petal by petal, to discover the fragrance and beauty within.

Group Activities for Kids who Hurt is about blossoming despite our many hurts, encouraging the pain to be the fertilizer that nurtures our growth and causes us to stretch beyond. It is not about fixing, for I believe not one of us is broken. It is about empowering, accessing the strength we each have within us to create a positive vision of who we want to be, and collectively supporting each other in reaching toward those dreams.

Contents

INTRODUCTION

A number of years ago as a school counselor, I was frequently contacted by teachers and community members who were serving in the role of facilitator for student assistance support groups. Although they were looking for lesson plans for a variety of groups, they had found a void when it came to materials for kids who were hurting. The leaders were full of compassion, skill and dedication, yet they lacked a plan. Group Activities for Kids Who Hurt is written in part to fill that void. If offers 15 comprehensive lesson plans for educational groups composed of children in third grade through eighth grade, who have issues around pain.

While writing Group Activities for Kids Who Hurt, I drew upon my 30 years spent leading groups and training others in group dynamics. I've also been fortunate to have gathered a wealth of experience as a longtime school counselor and teacher, a parent and foster parent, and licensed professional counselor in private practice. All of those experiences have influenced and enriched not only me, but this book as well. I particularly value the many kids who have helped me shape these activities; I recall their sad eyes brightening, "Ah ha." moments, hearts opening, and self-esteem growing strong and whole. It is this I wish for you and all of the kids you come to serve.

Initially Group Activities for Kids Who Hurt was to be organized in segments based on specific types of traumas or hurts that kids might have encountered: divorce and separation, loss of a loved one, alcohol and drug abuse, low self-esteem, teasing and bullying, and other poignant topics. However, as I reflected on many years of working with kids in pain, researched anew, and counseled directly with kids currently dealing with difficult issues, I became aware that hurt has a common denominator. Regardless of the cause of the pain, hurting shows up in a similar fashion. This awareness has played a significant role in shaping the format of this book.

Ideally, Group Activities for Kids Who Hurt is designed to harness the power of eclectic grouping, bringing kids together not only to be heard, but also to provide a support system for each other in the midst of their own hurting and healing. It is based on a premise that acknowledging hurt is only one critical step in the process of healing. Developing compassion, forgiveness and moving beyond the pain are other crucial steps that can be facilitated in the context of a group dynamic. With this in mind, the activities can be used sequentially, building on one another, with the assumption that the same students are attending the group for the whole approximately 15 weeks. However, the lessons are also written in such a way that they have significant value as stand-alone activities when that is more appropriate.

Before I go any further, I want to acknowledge that you already have tremendous expertise. You know the circumstances of your work with kids, know how to lead groups, and know the needs of your own population. In that light, Group Activities for Kids Who Hurt becomes a dynamic resource in which each activity standing alone can be powerful, enlightening and healing. I encourage you to use this book as you see fit, selecting what works best for you.

I also realize that you know there are great variations among kids, third through eighth grade. In selecting which activities from my repertoire to include in this book, I was particularly sensitive to include only those that I knew from experience would be successful across many levels and types of kids. As you lead the activities, it will be important to gear your language and approach not only to the appropriate age, but also to the ethnicity, and the socioeconomic and maturity level of the group. Once again, I honor your expertise and trust that you have many skills and talents with which you will be successful.

BENEFITS OF GROUP ACTIVITIES
FOR KIDS WHO HURT

One of my major goals in writing this book was to create lesson plans that are clear, concise, comprehensive and easy to use. There are other benefits for you, too.

First, if you choose to present the lessons in their entirety, you will enjoy their continuity. There will no longer be a need for scrambling week after week to figure out what's next for the group. Instead of a miscellaneous collection of activities that may or may not relate to one another, you are now armed with a sequential program.

Second, at a glance you can scan the lesson's objectives and a materials list so you know immediately why you will be presenting the lesson, and what supplies are needed. Also, each lesson starts with a prologue directed to you, the leader, providing valuable insight and information to prepare you for that specific lesson.

When it comes to actually guiding participants through the lessons, you have been given procedures in which you will find comprehensive yet simple action plans for each activity.

I also want to stress the value of the discussion questions. They are an important and powerful part of each lesson, geared to help the participants culminate their experience, integrate their learnings and bring them to cognition. Group members will walk away not only with a powerful experience, but with an awareness of their new knowledge.

Two final benefits are the reproducible Experience Sheets and Journal Pages, which are available for each participant after each lesson. These pages allow for quiet reflection and personal growth beyond the actual group lesson.

HOW TO USE THIS BOOK

It might be helpful for you to thumb through the pages for a moment and notice how this book is set up. There are three main sections. The first section is about getting started, which creates a solid foundation of communication, trust and group dynamics. The second section provides activities and discussion questions on topics that encourage moving through the hurt and into healing. The third and final section is specifically about closure.

The activities in each section have an identical structure designed to facilitate the group experience with ease. The structure looks like this:

Prologue: providing relevant information and inspiration offered directly to the leader

Objectives: what participants will experience and learn

Materials List: what you need for that lesson

Procedure: giving specific instructions and guidance on the lesson flow. This is the "What do I do?" and "How do I do it?" section. Included in Procedure are "You might say ..." suggestions, offered as possibilities to trigger your mind as the leader. Of course, you will want to reword these comments, using your own words and style.

Discussion Questions: part of what makes this book unique and powerful. The Discussion Questions help students to integrate not only what they did, but what impact it can have on them and their world at large. It answers: "What have I learned?"

Reproducible Experience Sheets and Journal Pages: supplemental to each group session. These have been designed to enhance the group experience both by providing reflective time between sessions, and offering alternate experiences relevant to group members. Participants take these personal, ungraded pages with them at the end of each group.

LEADERSHIP AND GROUP DYNAMICS

Leading groups is an art, in which natural talent may blossom, but skills can also be developed. It is certainly not necessary to be a professional counselor or therapist to lead wonderful groups. In fact, community volunteers who are willing to dedicate time and energy to facilitate groups often become superb leaders.

There are, however, some qualities and skills that tend to enhance the dynamic of a group, and that facilitators might profit by developing. Among the most important is an ability to listen emphatically, with focused attention, giving eye contact and exercising the blessing of having two ears and only one mouth. While listening, watch for nonverbal communication such as facial expressions and body language. Listen with your intuition as well as your mind. That "gut level understanding" is often very insightful. Validate the group members so they know you heard and understood. This can be done both verbally and nonverbally, and provides a sense of trust and comfort. It is also important to know how to help a speaker clarify thoughts, and to invite reflection.

While your primary goal in group facilitation may be to support the members, remember to take care of yourself, too. Set and keep healthy boundaries. Notice your own body language. It often provides a clue as to "What's happening now with me?" and offers an opportunity to help you develop a comfort level with conflict, intensity and silence. Accept some anxiety. It is normal. As you are real, authentic, genuine and honest, you will be able to acknowledge mistakes and successes. Offer love, respect and trust, even to yourself.

Remain impersonal, rather than personal, compassionate rather than sympathetic. The difference is about staying clear and of service, rather that trying to fix, and ending up taking it home with you.

Listen to the words you select and how you deliver them, especially by monitoring your tone of voice. This sets the stage for encouraging nonjudgmental feedback and responses from member to member. Also it is important to respond (responsibility), rather than react. Some helpful responses to model might be:

Tell me more ...   Sounds like ...

It seems to me ...   I get the feeling or impression that ...

I hear you saying ...   I wonder ...

I'm wondering if ...   As I hear it, you ...

Sometimes the most important thing you can do with your wisdom is to remain silent.

Perhaps these qualities and skills seem like a large bill to fill, and truly they are. It may help to keep in mind the potential of the group to positively affect the lives of others. It also helps to remember that you are there to support, not fix. Trust that the answers are inside of each group member. Your job is to nurture their self-discovery and self- healing, rather than to take control and attempt to change or fix.

It might be helpful to think of yourself as a guide who encourages new ways of thinking, feeling and behaving. Create a positive environment by providing structure, setting norms, establishing rules and confidentiality, eliciting accountability, creating safety, fostering learning and expression, supporting sharing, encouraging risk-taking, and promoting healing. All of this promotes positive self-esteem, which supports the members in applying what they learn to life situations. It may sound difficult, but believe it or not, you have already been developing these skills, which you use in forming relationships throughout life. Take inventory, and honor the vast experience you bring to the group. Let this knowledge be your safety net, then trust your heart.

Normal Group Stages:

There is one piece of knowledge that has helped me immensely as a group leader through the years. It is a model presenting normal group stages initially developed by B.W. Tuckman in the 1960s. Typical groups float into and out of these stages in a fairly predictable manner. When I notice a group in transition, or an awkward phase, it is very reassuring to remember this model.

Stage 1: Forming: This is about building trust. The main questions are "What's this all about and can I trust the others who are here?" Anxiety is prevalent in this stage. Just when the group seems to be settling in, and the leader is ready for a sigh of relief that all is well, it is time for a transition.

Stage 2: Storming: This is about acceptance and tends to be an anxious phase. There are often conflicts, agitation, whispering, complaining, vying for power, cliques and pairing up. The bad news is that some groups never get past this phase. The good news is that when they do, they make another transition. It is so helpful to remember, in the midst of this stage, that it is normal. Breathe deeply, allow group tension, give permission for the conflict, and love yourself.

> Plan to your heart's content, then be willing to surrender to the moment.

Stage 3: Norming: This is about harmony. Tension dissipates as the group comes together with a personality of its own. It is now able to focus and be a coherent body, moving into yet another transition.

Stage 4: Performing: This is about working together agreeably. Members are taking charge and moving forward harmoniously, reaching goals and supporting each other.

Stage 5: Celebration/Closure: This is about joy and termination, preparing for and accomplishing the transition out of the group. Although closure happens to be the final session, it is normal for participants to begin this stage early as they know the group is coming to an end. You may notice some withdrawal, or some clinging behaviors, as each person lets go in their own way.

Stage 6: Debriefing: This stage is specifically for the facilitator(s), and is done once the group has terminated. It provides a reflective opportunity to process feelings, thoughts, learnings and undone business, thus providing closure for the leaders. The following series of reflections may be helpful when debriefing yourself and thinking back on the entire group experience:

1. Take a moment to reflect back over the group experience, recalling your intentions for the group as well as your experience.
2. What stands out for you; what is most significant for you?
3. How does that connect to what is happening in your life now?
4. Listen inside yourself for guidance, blessing or wisdom to be offered to you. Create an affirmation out of what you hear.
5. What is the next step toward making that affirmation and/or guidance a reality in your life?
6. Visualize yourself taking that next step.
7. Acknowledge yourself.

> As facilitator I may grow the most, but don't tell my group members.

These reflections assist in letting go of the group process as well as participants. They help to acknowledge the experience, which can be as powerful for the facilitator as for the members. And they help the facilitator to release, let go and move on into whatever comes next in life.

Section I

Here you will find detailed plans for the first three sessions, focusing on getting to know one another, establishing group rules, setting goals, exploring the issues of pain and healing, and discovering the power of thought. It was written with the intent that groups would do these three sessions in order to establish trust and a group dynamic conducive to the next weeks of constructive growth.

A Positive Beginning

The first day of a group is largely about getting to know one another, establishing ground rules and clear expectations, beginning to develop trust, finding some points of commonality, and creating space for individuality. It's a time to elicit some depth, without being too scary.

Day one is different than the others in terms of structure. Instead of one long activity, you will find three separate shorter ones that together take approximately an hour. If your first session is shorter than an hour, or if you have more sessions than the 15 allotted, it would be possible to divide these three activities into two separate days. It is important, however, to keep the three activities in the given order.

> Piglet sidled up to Pooh from behind. "Pooh!" he whispered.
> "Yes, Piglet?"
> "Nothing," said Piglet, taking Pooh's paw. "I just wanted to be sure of you."
> A. A. Milne

Awareness Check

Prologue:

It is not uncommon at the start of a group for members to have mixed feelings and thoughts about being there. Anxiety tends to be high, especially in a group in which members do not know each other. This activity provides a starting place for discussion and sharing. It helps to focus the attention on the present, being in the group, and eliciting a sense of belonging and commitment to stay.

As facilitator, you can set the tone for the day with a warm and friendly welcome. Invite members to sit in a circle and share names. Name tags can be useful too.

In your own words you might say something like: "Welcome to Group. Although you are all unique and different, you have some things in common, too. One of them is that you have decided to come to a group for kids who hurt because you are having or have had some painful experiences in your life. You are all here to learn some ways to begin to heal from your hurt. We will be doing activities together, sharing and learning to give and receive support from each other.

"Although we will be working together, we will also have fun while we learn. We will be meeting for 15 weeks at this same time and place for an hour. It is important to come to each session, and I'm very glad you're here today. Before we leave today we will talk more about group expectations and have time for questions, but for now, let's jump into our first activity."

Approximate Time: 15 minutes

Objectives:

Group members will:
*   begin the process of building group trust
*   discover that they are not alone in their hurting
*   find common ground with other members
*   assess their own states of mind and willingness to be in group

Materials:

Paper
Pencils or pens
Chart paper and markers or whiteboard

Procedure:

Ask each participant to jot down brief answers to four questions below. Let them know ahead of time that they will be invited to share, but they may choose to keep the answers private. Also, they may decide to draw a quick sketch instead of use words. After each question, give about a minute for the participants to write or sketch silently. The four questions are:
*   What are you thinking about?
*   What are you feeling?
*   What worries or expectations have you brought with you?
*   What would you rather be doing right now?

Invite members to share their answers, while you record the responses on a board or chart paper.

Discussion Questions:

1. What have you learned or discovered about the group?
2. What have you learned or discovered about yourself?
3. What similarities and differences do you see?
4. How is it possible to want to be in a group and not in a group at the same time?

Creating Group Rules

Prologue:

Once the group has completed the Awareness Check, the members will be armed and ready to create group rules. They will have had an opportunity to talk, and understand the importance of listening. They will know how important it is to share without worrying about others laughing at them or telling their stories outside of group. They will understand why each person needs to have a turn, but that no one should be forced to take one. In other words, they will see the value of respecting each other.

> "To be loved, be lovable."
>
> Ovid

Approximate time: 15 minutes

Objectives:

Group members will:
* discuss what would make them feel safe in the group
* discuss what would make the group work well
* brainstorm possible group rules
* select and agree on a list of five or six rules
* write the list on poster board to save for each session
* sign the rules sheet as a commitment to follow them

Materials:

Pencils or pens
Chart paper and markers or whiteboard
One sheet poster board
Journal page for each group member

Procedure:

You might say: "What do you think would be useful to make this group feel like a safe and warm place where you could feel comfortable to share? What would it take to make you want to come back each week? How should we behave? Let's brainstorm a list of ideas for some guidelines or rules. Remember, in a brainstorm, all of the answers can be written down, then we will go back and look at them together."

Step 1: Using the whiteboard or chart paper to record the results for all to see, brainstorm a list of ideas for guidelines or rules.

Step 2: Review the list together and circle those rules that the group agrees are most important.

Step 3. Write the final list on poster board to have available for each session.

Step 4: Ask each group member to sign the poster to indicate agreement, acceptance and willingness to follow the rules.

Step 5: Pass out a Journal page to each group member. Allow time for everyone to copy the rules onto their sheets.

Suggested rules might include:
*   Outside of group I can talk about myself, but I will not talk about anyone else's experience that was shared in the group (confidentiality).
*   Everyone gets to take turns, so time is shared.
*   It is OK to pass.
*   We listen to the person who is sharing, and speak one at a time.
*   We are respectful of ourselves and each other.
*   I will be on time.

Discussion Questions:

1. Why will it be important for each of us to follow the rules?
2. Even though we often don't like rules, sometimes they are needed. Why is that true in a group?
3. What might happen if group members choose to ignore the rules?

Goal Setting

Prologue:

One of the best ways to ensure success in a group is to encourage members to set their own personal goals. Goal setting fuels enthusiasm, which leads to more cooperation in group process as well as action. The group experience becomes richer and more productive.

Approximate time: 20 minutes

Objectives:

Group members will:
* understand the long-range plan for the group
* be introduced to the importance of goal setting
* set individual goals to enhance the group experience and record them on their Experience Sheets.

Materials:

Experience Sheet, "My Goals," for each member

Procedure:

At this point, give a brief overview of the long-range plan for the group. Explain that the group will run 15 sessions once a week (or another plan, if appropriate). Briefly mention some of the upcoming topics, introduce the Experience Sheets and Journal pages. Share how they are designed to be reflective, ungraded and enjoyable. You might emphasize that they are provided as tools to help group members deal with their own struggles.

You might then ask: "Can anyone think of why it could be a good idea to set goals for yourself as a way to make your time in this group valuable?" Encourage answers that focus on the importance of setting individual goals in order to profit fully from the group experience by committing to the group process, to the other individuals in the group, and especially to personal growth.

Then ask: "What sorts of things might be included in a goal setting list?" Ideas are: showing up for each group, arriving on time, writing each Journal entry, doing Experience Sheets, and following the rules created by the group.

Discussion Questions:

1. What is a goal?
2. Why do we need them?
3. In what way will they help us?

After the brief discussion, pass out the Experience Sheets. Ask the group members to take these with them to complete and bring back for the next session.

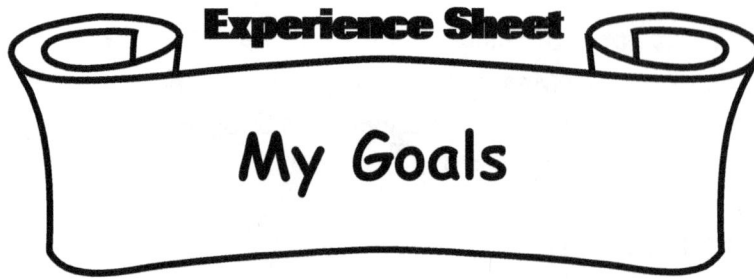

Experience Sheet

My Goals

Name_____ Date_____

My goals for this group are:

_____

_____

_____

_____

_____

I will work toward these goals by:

_____

_____

_____

_____

I am willing to contribute to this group by:

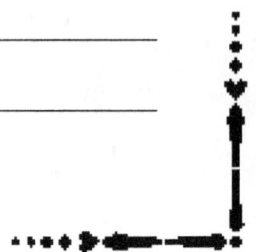

_____

_____

_____

_____

My Journal

Write the group rules in your journal. Add your signature and today's date to show your agreement with the rules.

_____

_____

_____

_____

_____

_____

_____

_____

_____

_____

Name _____ Date _____

Recall your group experience. Write about your thoughts, feelings and reactions.

_____

_____

_____

_____

"Those who set goals create their own futures."
James Fadiman

_____

Healing Hurt and Pain

Prologue:

This meeting of the group is a "getting down to business" day in terms of our topic, "Hurt." Art Exploration provides an opportunity for group members to sculpt their pain, making it concrete, tactile. They get to know it, feel it, and discover how it is manageable. In addition, while sharing whatever pieces of the pain they choose to disclose, they see that they are not alone in the hurting, nor do they need to stay lonely. The final metaphor of putting pain to rest, in its tactile form, literally into the container, is a way to acknowledge "I can contain this hurt."

I can handle it.

Objectives:

Group members will:
* begin to define their hurt
* explore and express feelings in a tactile manner
* sculpt or draw their hurt
* share with one other person
* learn more about the other group members

Materials:

Play-Doh™ or a similar substance. The Play-Doh™ can be purchased in containers, labeled for each group member, and given to them at the end of the session. Another idea is to make a homemade patch of playdough (see recipe at end of activity) and store it in individually labeled plastic bags. Each member will then have some to take home.

Note:

Crayons and drawing paper can be used instead of Play-Doh™. However, the activity loses the impact provided by the three-dimensional aspect of molding and shaping the hurt.

Procedure:

At the end of of the first meeting, group members took their Experience Sheets with them to work on individual goals. They were instructed to bring them back today. At the start of session today, invite members to talk briefly about the parts of the goal-setting sheet they feel comfortable sharing. If time is not an issue, this could be done in the large group. However, if time is limited, members can pair up to be more time-efficient. In either case, this provides an important opportunity for them to verbalize their goals and receive support from their peers.

Once the sharing is done, give each group member a container or handful of playdough. Briefly introduce the concept that feeling pain or hurt is a normal human response to an unhappy experience, and that in this group hurt and pain is something everyone is experiencing to some degree. Ask them to imagine what their pain would look like if it had a shape that they could hold in their hands. Invite them to use the next five to seven minutes to individually sculpt a model of their hurt or pain. (The alternative is to draw; see previous note.) Be sure to tell the group members they will be sharing their art when done, and that there are no right or wrong answers.

> I shape my relationship to my hurt.

When time is up, ask them to silently hold their art extended outwardly in their hands then mill around showing their sculpture and looking at one anothers' work.

After a minute or so, ask each member to pair up with one other person whose work they were drawn to for some reason, perhaps curiosity, similarity to their own, etc. (A group of three can work if there is an odd number.) Ask them to review their partners' names, then share about their art. Suggest they talk about what it means, why they chose it, or how they feel about it. This takes about three minutes per person.

Bring the group back together and have partners introduce each other, sharing one thing they learned about their partners from the art exploration.

If using playdough or Play-Doh™, have the members return it to the containers to keep. Other forms of art could be collected and kept to look back at later.

Discussion Questions:

1. When we sculpt or draw our hurts or struggles, we can shape them however we want to. In real life, are there ways we can shape our pain?

2. What was it like to find other group members with feelings similar to yours? How about different feelings?

3. If you were to reshape your art to express how you would feel without the pain, what might it look like?

Playdough Recipe

In a saucepan, mix:
1 cup flour
1/2 cup salt
2 teaspoons cream of tartar
1 tablespoon vegetable oil
1 cup water

While stirring, cook over medium heat until consistency of playdough. Scrape saucepan as you turn the playdough on to a work surface. Knead in the food colorings of your choice. Makes approximately 16 portions.

Experience Sheet

How I Feel

Today in your group session, you had a chance to make a playdough shape or draw a picture of your hurt or pain. You also talked about how you would like to feel, if you had the power to change.

Imagine how you will feel when you are no longer feeling the sadness or pain. In the space below, draw how that will feel. It is ok to make your artwork as fancy or as simple as you like. You can use lots of colors, too.

As you look at your finished picture, what is one word that you could use to describe it?

Write it here: _____

Think of one thing you can do right now to feel more like your picture. Draw a Happy Face when you've done it.

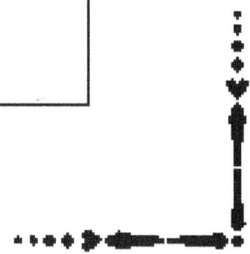

My Journal

Write a letter to your hurt.

"Dear Hurt, Today I ... "

_____

_____

_____

_____

_____

_____

_____

_____

_____

_____

_____

Recall your group experience. Write about your thoughts, feelings and reactions.

_____

_____

_____

_____

_____

"I've always believed that you can think positive just as well as you can think negative."
Sugar Ray Robinson

_____

S-T-O-P That Thought

Prologue:

The major concept presented in this session is perhaps the most critical of all. It is pivotal in grasping control of our immediate world, for each of us lives within a world created by our thinking. In a nutshell, it is: "As we think, so we become."

This session works with the following powerful key: What we hold in our minds makes all the difference about how we eventually feel. This doesn't necessarily mean that we will immediately recover from a hurt by changing our thinking, but that changed thinking can help heal a person in time.

By taking responsibility for our thinking, we can also step out of a victim role. Think of healing a scraped knee. If the scab is continually picked, the wound cannot heal. So it is with hurts; it is not constructive to hash out old hurts. It leaves a bigger scar. Instead, we promote healing with a positive self-image created out of positive thinking, thus developing inner strengths that can handle hurts.

> "Let the sadness die out for lack of attention."
> Pegge Butenhoff

Objectives:

Group members will:
* learn a model for halting negative thinking patterns
* practice the model
* brainstorm recurring thoughts they would like to stop
* decide on a specific thought pattern to S-T-O-P in daily life

Materials:

Copies of the S-T-O-P That Thought model for each member
Red construction paper
Scissors

Procedure:

Lead a discussion of how thoughts can go around and around in our heads, even when we want them to stop. Give some examples of these "sticky" thoughts: (I can't ..., I'll never be enough ..., Nobody likes me ..., This hurt will never end ...). Ask for others to share examples of their own.

Then you might say, "Each of you has come to the group because you are dealing with something hurtful in your life. We're here to talk about life, because for each of us it is full of pain and celebration. This may not be the best time of your life, but things can change and be different. People come out of all kinds of adversity and struggles to become stronger and more healthy. How do they do that? One way is to change their thinking.

"Did you know that as you think, you become? You may not be able to change what's already happened, but you can change the way you feel about the events by changing how you think about them.

"It helps to focus on what you want your life to be like, things you like, talents you have, things you are good at, what service you can offer. Do this instead of focusing on the negative, the hurtful emotions, situations and feelings. Look for things of interest in your life, for example, find books about things you like, play sports, draw, or spend time with friends. Keep your focus and your thoughts on the things you enjoy and that bring you good feelings.

"So today we're going to do an activity that will help us to grasp some control over our thinking. It's called: S-T-O-P That Thought ."

Introduce the S-T-O-P That Thought model as a method for stopping a sticky thought process and replacing it with something more favorable.

Pass out and read the S-T-O-P That Thought model.

Brainstorm some sticky thoughts that might be helped by this model.

> Life is full of pain and celebration. Where do you choose to place your attention?

Practice aloud with a few examples.

Each group member then cuts out a red stop sign and pastes the S-T-O-P That Thought model on it to keep as a reminder of the S-T-O-P process.

Discussion Questions:

1. How do those sticky thoughts first get stuck in our heads?
2. In what way does praising ourselves help to change our thinking?
3. What is the one and only thing in life we can control? (Our thoughts) Explain.
4. If we don't control our thinking, who else does?
5. How can I change my thinking to feel good about myself?

Extension Activity:

Role plays are such an important way to experience and rehearse behavioral changes. If time allows, try role-playing some of the negative thought patterns along with the S-T-O-P That Thought model. See how they come alive when acted out.

"Whether you think you can, or that you can't, you are usually right."

Henry Ford

When you have negative thinking, use this process...

S-T-O-P That Thought

Stop when you become aware of a sticky thought.

Then rephrase the thought into more helpful words.

Over and over again repeat the new thought.

Praise yourself for changing your thinking.

"Your words create what you speak about. Learn to speak positively."
Sanaya Roman

Feeling Good About Me

How do you feel about yourself when you believe someone doesn't like you?

_____

_____

How do you feel about yourself when you know someone cares about you?

_____

_____

If you think of someone as being more important than you are, how can you change your thinking so you feel important, too? This will help you stop giving your power away.

_____

_____

One way to feel better about yourself is to find a way to help other people. You might help someone with their homework, volunteer to help out with chores at home, or read to a younger brother or sister. Pick out and do something for someone else, then write a short description or draw a picture below of the action you chose to take.

What is one word that describes how you feel now? _____

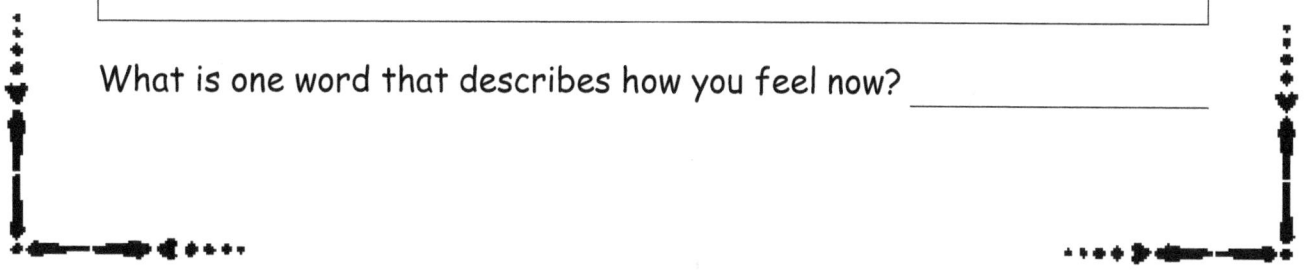

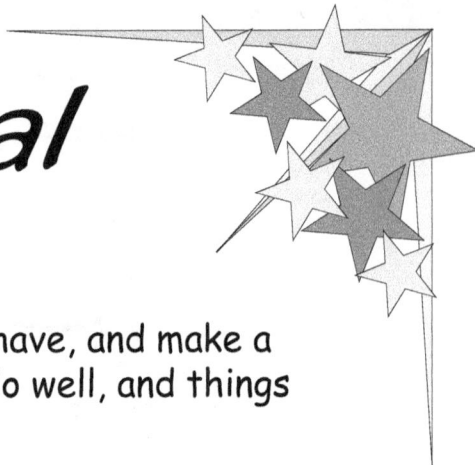

My Journal

Focus on some of the good qualities that you have, and make a list. It might help to think about things you do well, and things about you that you are proud of.

_____

_____

_____

_____

_____

_____

_____

_____

_____

Recall your group experience. Write about your thoughts, feelings and reactions.

_____

_____

_____

_____

_____

"No one can make you feel inferior without your consent."
Eleanor Roosevelt

_____

Section II

     Provided here are lesson plans for sessions covering the topics of Anger; Forgiveness; Kindness, Compliments and Affirmations; The Body-Mind Connection; Compassion, Humor and Joy; Grief and Loss; Goal Setting and Service. Although designed to be used sequentially, there is some freedom of choice within this section. At your discretion as leader, and given time constraints, some sessions might be eliminated if they do not seem relevant or essential to a specific group of kids. Also, as discussed previously, these lessons can each stand alone.

Managing Anger

Prologue:

In general when things go differently than the way we want them to, or if we are feeling afraid or hurt, anger is one common response. Festering anger builds walls, isolates us from positive opportunities, and keeps us from feeling whole. It can also prevent us from dealing with underlying feelings, thus creating extra baggage to be carried around.

I find it most helpful to consider anger as a messenger, a signal that there is something about me that I need to change . That attitude steers me away from wanting to blame, feeling a lack of self-control or loss of personal power. Listening to my anger as a signal has helped me so much in my life. Instead of staying angry at others or things, I now most often can quickly notice my anger and immediately tune in to what about me I need to change. I seldom work myself into a rage anymore, and hardly even a hot temper. I am much more balanced because I no longer give away my center, my personal power or my energy by being angry. It just doesn't serve.

The flip side of anger is fear, so helpful questions for me to ask when I become aware of my anger are: "What am I afraid to lose?" and "What am I afraid I will not gain?" These questions are also useful when leading groups. If I notice anger and resistance among participants, perhaps there is something I can do to lower the fear factor and create more safety. Often this will defuse the resistance or anger.

Objectives:

Group members will:
* understand how thinking triggers the anger response
* identify typical anger-producing situations and reactions
* identify consequences of various reactions/responses to anger
* identify and practice ways to alter thinking to manage anger

Materials:

Whiteboard, or chart paper and markers

Procedure:

You might say: " All of us get angry from time to time, especially when feeling hurt or threatened in some way. A common response to being hurt is to want to blame someone else, to strike out at others and things, or to feel resentful. Those reactions can leave us feeling negative and out of control.

"Today we are going to consider a new approach to anger, especially as it relates to the pain and hurt that brought each member to this group. It is an approach that encourages us to manage anger in positive ways by changing our thinking about the events and/or people that we choose to get angry at. Yes, anger is a choice; we can control it rather than it controlling us."

At the top of a chart paper or column on the board write: "What it feels like to be angry." Ask group members to tell about how they feel when they are angry. How do their bodies, minds and emotions feel? Many of the responses will probably describe physical reactions. Record responses on the board or chart paper.

At the top of another chart paper or on a new column on the board write, "How I react when angry." Ask group members to brainstorm typical reactions they have when angry, in other words, what they do when angry. These responses will describe behaviors.

At the top of the third chart paper or third column on the board, write, "Situations that trigger anger." Suggest they think about any anger that may be related to the issues that led them to group, and to consider if these hurtful issues are triggers for angry responses. You might say, "Remember I mentioned earlier that when we hurt, we often react with anger and blame, and we want to strike out. Are any of the hurtful situations in your life triggering your anger? Tell us more about that ..." Again record these. When you are done brainstorming, you will have three charts headed like this:

What it feels like to be angry ...	How I react when angry ...	Situations that trigger anger ...

Now have group members look back at the three charts and decide on one situation to work with in a role play.

The member who owns the angry situation will prompt one or more other participants as to their roles in the role play. Instruct them to act out the situation from the beginning up until the anger is first triggered. At that point, stop the role play. Caution: Avoid acting out any angry or ugly encounters. Role play is a powerful tool that helps internalize behaviors. We only want to internalize positive behaviors.

Ask the group members to become aware of possible negative thinking that may be feeding the anger. In other words, what thoughts are leading to the anger?

Introduce the idea of anger as a messenger, a signal that there is something about the angry person that needs to change when they become angry. What is the message the anger brings? And what could be changed to manage the situation? (Remember, they are not trying to change someone else, but to change the thinking that leads to the reaction of anger.)

Discuss positive responses and ways of thinking that could help to resolve the situation without blame and anger. The group decides on one suggested solution, then the role play is resumed to act out the positive response. (Caution: It is important to focus on acting out the positive rather that practicing any negative behaviors.)

Repeat this process with several other brainstormed situations. Each time, the goal is to catch the negative thinking or reacting and see how it could be changed to yield more positive results.

Discussion Questions:

1. Is anger ever justified? How or how not?
2. In what ways can it be appropriate to feel anger, express it, and still behave in a constructive way?
3. In what ways are anger and fear related?
4. What were some of the times when you acted angry because you were scared?

A Favorite Place

Sometimes when you feel angry, it helps to have a few positive images in your mind that you can use to help control or stop the anger. This exercise will help you create your own mental image of a safe and peaceful place that you can visit mentally whenever you like.

Imagine walking down a trail to a favorite place where you feel happy and safe. When you reach the favorite place in your mind, imagine yourself there, enjoying it with all of your senses. Smell its smells, taste its tastes, touch it, feel it and see yourself in it. Let it become as real to you as possible. In fact, if it is an actual physical place, go take a picture of it for your journal. You might want to draw or paint the picture instead. Once this place is very real in your mind, it can become a wonderful spot to travel to mentally when you need time out from hurt or conflict. Just close your eyes, and feel its safety and joy.

Write a short description of your favorite place or draw a picture of it:

Think of a word that describes how you feel about your favorite place. Write it here: _____

My Journal

As you've been learning in group, by changing your thoughts, you can change your feelings. It helps to be prepared with some positive thoughts that make you happy and lift you up when you're feeling down.

Think about things that make you feel good. Write about them here. Some examples are: a favorite song, movie or book, a sport you like, special people, a hot bubble bath, wearing certain clothes, running around the block, hitting tennis balls, happy memories, etc. Include things you can do without others, so you aren't dependent on someone else to help you feel good. Keep your list to look at when you're feeling blue.

_____

_____

_____

_____

_____

_____

Recall your group experience. Write about your thoughts, feelings and reactions.

_____

_____

_____

"A man becomes what he thinks about most of the time."
Ralph Waldo Emerson

_____

Learning to Forgive

Special Note:

This is a two-part activity. Both parts can be done on the same day.

Prologue:

A revelation happened for me the day I realized that when I forgive another person, the forgiveness is not for them; it really is for me. When I carry around hurt, blame, resentment, anger, fear, etc., it can feel like rocks in a backpack. Forgiveness is about unloading my backpack so that I may live lighter and more freely. In fact, the other person involved may not even know I am carrying it. If they do, they may not care. Whatever their reaction is, it doesn't matter. The point is, if I have something to forgive, it is my problem. If I choose not to forgive, my lack of forgiveness poisons the world in which I live.

I have discovered that even if I have been wrongly treated, I can forgive. I do not have to believe that the other person was right, because I do have a right to know my boundaries. I do not even have to verbally share my forgiveness with the other person. I may not even ever see him or her again. But I can rid my consciousness of the feelings and thoughts that need to be released; I can forgive inside myself.

You might think of it this way: If my backpack is full of rocks that weigh me down, there is no room for me to receive the many wonderful opportunities and gifts that the world has to give. Forgiving creates space. Also, remember that I get what I give. So if I can give kindness and gentleness by forgiving, then kindness, gentleness and forgiveness can come back to me.

> Forgiveness gives us an opportunity for a clean slate.

Part 1

Objectives:

Group members will:
* see how hurtful words leave strong impressions
* recall a time when they hurt someone's feelings
* develop an awareness of how hard it can be to eliminate hurts
* see a need for forgiving and letting go

Materials:

Two sheets of paper for each member
Pencils or pens

Procedure:

Invite the group members to each think of a friend, then remember a time that he or she had hurt the friend's feelings in some way. Give the group a few minutes to think, then ask for a couple of volunteers to share.

Next, have the group members each write the name of one of their friends on a piece of paper and wad it up in a ball. Then have them try to smooth out the wrinkles; some will remain.

Ask, "What do those wrinkles represent?" Responses will be along the lines of: "Once you hurt a friend, it is impossible to take those words or behaviors back; they will leave an impact (wrinkles)."

Invite members to recall a time when they were hurt by someone, write the name of that person on a sheet of paper, then wrinkle it up, too. Have them try to smooth out the wrinkles; some will remain.

> If I truly forgive, I can't look back and remember what the problem was.

Again ask, "What do those wrinkles represent?" Responses will be along the lines of: "Once someone hurts me, it is hard to make the hurt go away. It shows how I still remember."

Ask participants to keep their wrinkled papers for now, as you move into Part 2.

Part 2:

Objectives:

Group members will:
* learn a method to forgive
* practice the forgiveness method
* let go of the hurt represented in Part 1

Materials:

Wrinkled papers from Part I
A trash can
A few pink roses with the thorns removed

Note:

If money allows, it is a wonderful touch to let each person keep a pink rose at the end of the session on this day.

Procedure:

Bring a few pink roses with the thorns removed to the group. Let each group member touch them, smell them, all velvety soft and tender. Allow time for them to create a vivid picture and sense of "pink rose."

Now ask members to close their eyes and think of a hurt they would like to forgive, perhaps the one they wrote down and wrinkled earlier.

Have them imagine the face of the person who created the hurt, and see themselves standing before that person. Imagine bowing, and remembering that even if they are still hurt or angry, the intention is to forgive.

Then have them imagine handing the other person pink roses. They can give the roses over and over. At first, the other person may not take the rose, or might even turn away. This indicates that the group member has not totally forgiven him/her yet. Encourage the member to keep handing out pink roses until the roses are accepted.

Note:

As facilitator, you may say: "You may find, for big hurts, that you need to repeat this exercise over and over before you are able to give a pink rose bouquet. Remember, it is worth the work. You are the one holding the lack of forgiveness, so you are the one to profit from the success."

Once they are done giving pink roses to the other people, they can also imagine their own faces, bow, and give pink roses to themselves, too.

Before they open their eyes, suggest they rub their eyes and stretch.

Ask if anyone wants to share.

Before closure, invite members to shred and throw away their wrinkled papers with names. Tell them this indicates that forgiveness can truly happen.

Discussion Questions:

1. How do you feel about closing your eyes and imagining?
2. What were you thinking about that helped you feel that way?
3. Why is it important to give yourself roses?
4. Are you aware of any different feelings or thoughts about the person you forgave or gave roses to? If so, what?
5. How might you use this exercise at home?

Throw Away Problems

Think about a problem you are dealing with now or have in the past. Now imagine that you can hold the problem in your hands. Imagine the faces of all the people involved, including your own face. As you hold the problem in your hands, send the problem love and positive thoughts. Really concentrate. Keep sending love and positive thoughts for a minute or two. Now throw the problem away by tossing it into the air and letting it drift away. Fill your hands again with wonderful love, and give yourself a big hug.

How do you feel now that you've done the exercise? Write it here.

_____

_____

_____

_____

_____

Write down some other problems you have that you could use this exercise with.

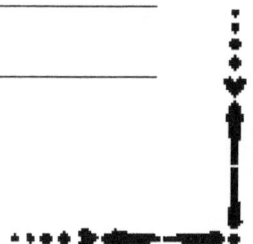

_____

_____

_____

_____

_____

My Journal

Write about: "A time I forgave another person."

_____

_____

_____

_____

_____

_____

_____

_____

_____

Recall your group experience. Write about your thoughts, feelings and reactions.

_____

_____

_____

_____

_____

"Forgiveness is the fragrance that the flower sheds upon the heel that crushed it."
Mark Twain

_____

Kindness, Compliments and Affirmations

Prologue:

Many kids who are hurting desperately want others to affirm them, saying somehow that they are "Ok." Although they hunger for kindness and gentleness, they often are mean and cruel to others. Perhaps this is a defensive behavior because they feel vulnerable. Perhaps it is born out of resentment that lingers from past hurts. Despite the cause, this negative outpouring of energy is harmful and self-defeating. When it bounces back to them, it creates more pain and suffering.

Even worse is the way they treat themselves. The negative language that plays in their heads can be full of put-downs, self-blame and unworthiness. It is often a habitual response to reject any compliments or kindnesses from others, and never to say anything good about themselves.

As a result, the subconscious mind is so full of negativity that it becomes chronically depressed and stifled. It is no wonder that kids who hurt often have very poor self-esteem and low self-worth.

The way to turn this negativity around is to change the thinking. This session focuses on ways to support positive thinking, to affirm, act and become more positive. It is about learning to be nice to others and oneself, and to say and do affirming things, rather than give out hurt or insults.

This session plants the seeds of kindness, which can blossom throughout the following weeks. I encourage you to come back to it often, reminding the group members and, especially, modeling these lessons for them and yourself.

> What you give to others, comes back to you.

Objectives:

Group members will:
*   reflect on positive qualities of the group personality
*   reflect on their own individual positive qualities
*   affirm the group through poetry
*   affirm themselves through poetry
*   make an affirming collage to keep in the group room

Materials:

Positive Poem format written on chart paper

Pencils or pens

2 poster boards (depending on the size of the group, maybe more)

Positive Poem Experience Sheets for each group member

Construction paper cut into one balloon shape per piece of paper, one per member

Procedure:

Ask the members to notice how the group has developed a personality of its own. Discuss what that personality is like; how would they describe it? What are some of its positive qualities? List these on the board.

Examples of qualities the group might share are: safety, fun, trustworthiness, doing new things, taking risks together, supportiveness, and coolness.

Display the format for a Positive Poem, which you have prewritten on chart paper. Read the example out loud a couple of times, exploring how it fits the model. Emphasize that it states only positive information about its subject, Toni Ann.

Next, together create a Positive Poem about the personality of the group, using the list of qualities generated earlier. Encourage discussion along the way, and especially monitor for no put-downs. You might brainstorm one line at a time, then write the completed group poem on poster board to display for future group sessions.

Positive Poem Format

One: name	Toni
Two: a positive phrase that describes	Enthusiastic about dancing
Three: is determined to	Will dance on stage one day
Four: four feeling words	Energetic, creative, joyful, strong
Five: proud of	Proud of taking risks
Six: succeeds in	Succeeds in being a good friend
Seven: loves these three things or people	Loves Bob, Josh and ice cream
Eight: gives in these three ways	Supports, comforts and believes
Nine: dreams about	Dreams of sandy beaches
Ten: restate or rephrase name	Toni Ann

> "The sweetest of all sounds is praise."
> Xenophon

After the group poem is complete, give each person a copy of the Experience Sheet with the poem format. Instruct each individual to write a Positive Poem about him- or herself on the Experience Sheet, then copy it onto the balloon-shaped paper. Encourage the group to share ideas and be supportive of each other. This is the time to relax and appreciate themselves.

When the balloons are all complete, group members paste them onto a large poster board, creating a collage of Positive Poems to display at future sessions.

Discussion Questions:

1. In what ways was it hard or easy to think of positive things about the group?
2. In what ways was it hard or easy to think of positive things about yourself?
3. Where do we get the thoughts and feelings we have about ourselves?
4. Do we have a right to change those feelings? Explain.

Positive Poem

Follow the directions for each line, and you will create a Positive Poem about the one and only YOU!

_____

(My name)

_____

(A positive phrase that describes me)

_____

(I am determined to ...)

_____ _____ _____ and _____

(Four feeling words that describe me)

_____

(I am proud of ...)

_____

(I succeed in ...)

_____ , _____ , _____

(I love these three things or people)

_____ , _____ , _____

(I give in these three ways)

_____

(I dream about ...)

_____

(My name restated or rephrased)

Positive Thinking

It can take a great deal of practice to turn our negative thinking around, into something more kind and gentle. Here are some fun ideas that may help you.

1. "Anonymous" means that no one knows who did it. Each day this week find three anonymous kind acts you can do, and do them. Some examples are: Pick up and throw away trash you find, put a nickel in a parking meter that is running out of time, make a friendly card and leave it on a friend's desk, set the table at home. Write some examples here of what you can do.

_____   _____

_____   _____

_____   _____

2. Look into your eyes in the mirror each day and say to yourself: "I love you." This is a wonderful way to erase some of the old negative messages you might have given yourself.

3. Write a short statement that is a positive message to yourself. This is called an "affirmation." Once you write it, repeat it to yourself all week, at least seven times a day. An example might be: "I am friendly and likable."

Write your affirmation here: _____

_____

_____

_____

_____

My Journal

Think about things in your life that you are feeling positive about right now. They may include ways you feel, things you're good at, things you've done that you're proud of, talents that you have, or other positive things. Write a list of them here.

_____

_____

_____

_____

_____

_____

_____

_____

Recall your group experience. Write about your thoughts, feelings and reactions.

_____

_____

_____

_____

"If you want to be happy, think happy thoughts."

_____

The Body-Mind Connection

Although this topic will be addressed in two sessions, we are just touching the tip of the iceberg. The connection between the body, mind and emotions has been researched and practiced for centuries. One school of thought teaches that everything we need is inside of us, and that we live inside of our bodies. If we adopt that belief momentarily, it's clear that developing a relationship with our bodies is vital. When we have body awareness of "what's happening now?" we can harness it to get through painful times by moving into the body for stress relief and support.

Emotions and memories tend to get stored in the body, and can cause a great deal of stress and "dis-ease." Unattended, these can lead to disease and depression. When the body is honored, emotions and old memories can be released, causing more freedom and health. There are many ways to defuse the stress stored in the body. These activities are two that I have used successfully for years. I encourage you to enjoy them, play with them, take them lightly, and to celebrate your body while leading the kids in enjoying the experience, too.

> "Angels fly because they take themselves lightly."
> G. K. Chesterton

Self-Massage

Prologue:

Self-Massage is designed to be introduced and lead by the facilitator, then given out later in the form of the Experience Sheet. Self-Massage is helpful for expending excess energy if the body feels too hyper, or for raising energy levels when the body is tired. In addition to being fun and relaxing, Self-Massage may increase feelings of alertness and joy. I've found that kids of all ages love it. They can practice it on their own. It's easy and fun to do, and has wonderful benefits, both mental and physical. Once it has been practiced a few times, it only takes minutes, so it might become an excellent warm-up or tension-breaker for future sessions.

Objectives:

Group members will:
* experience the practice of Self-Massage
* practice a set of movements for stress relief
* become aware of their bodies
* celebrate the self in the body

Materials:

One leader's copy of the Self-Massage Experience Sheet
Self-Massage Experience Sheets for each member

Procedure:

Have the group members stand, perhaps moving chairs to the sides of the room to create space. Make sure each person has sufficient room in which to move comfortably. Ask the group members to close their eyes for a moment, breathe deeply and be aware of their bodies. Instruct them to open their eyes, and begin to lead the Self-Massage from the Experience Sheet. Remember, have fun with it. The idea is to de-stress.

Celebrate your body.

At the end of the experience, find places to sit, maybe on the floor close together. Respond to comments or questions. Close this session by giving the group members copies of the Experience Sheet. Discuss how they might continue to use the activity.

Discussion Questions:

1. What do you notice about your body now that is different from before you experienced Self-Massage?
2. How do our bodies "talk" to us?
3. If you noticed any places in your body that were tender, what messages might those places have been telling you?
4. Why is it important to listen to our bodies?

Self-Massage

1. Standing up, stretch your arms in the air and reach toward the sky.

2. Make fists and bring your hands down to pound the top of your head, and all around the sides and back, onto your neck. You can do it hard or gently.

3. Now pull on your ears from top to bottom with your fingers and thumb. How big can you stretch your ears?

4. Take your index finger and rub right in front of your ears until you feel heat, then gently play drums on your cheeks with your fingers.

6. Pinch the bridge of your nose, right where glasses would sit, then rub your temples in a circle to relax your head.

7. Softly make circles with two fingers on your eyes, then press gently for a few seconds (or minutes if you like), and watch your inner sky.

8. Hammer your mouth with fingertips, then open it and make sounds.

9. Shake out your hands as you feel that you are shaking off tension and energy.

10. Use the fist of your right hand to pound up and down on your left shoulder, lifting your right elbow in front of you so you can reach further down onto your back. Then use your left hand on your right shoulder. Pound up your neck at the same time.

11. Use your fists to pound your chest while you make Tarzan sounds.

12. Now take your fists to pound down your arms, first on the outside, then inside, several times each.

13. Twist and pull each finger including your thumbs, one by one. Shake out your hands.

14. Pound three lines down your thighs, the center, inside and outside.

15. Now lean forward and pound your back and buttocks, especially where your blue jean pockets would be located. It's ok to giggle.

16. Stand up straight again and stretch to the sky.

17. Bring your hands together and clap for how wonderful you are.

My Journal

Write about: My body is my friend because ...

_____

_____

_____

_____

_____

_____

_____

_____

_____

_____

Recall your group experience. Write about your thoughts, feelings and reactions.

_____

_____

_____

_____

"There's only one corner of the universe you can be certain of improving: and that's your own self."

Aldous Huxley

_____

Affirm Your Body!

Prologue:

Many times the messages we give our bodies are quite sad. It is not uncommon to hear comments like: "I am so fat," "I am so skinny," "I am so clumsy," "I can't do anything," "I wish I could look like ...," "Why can't I be (taller, stronger, shorter, prettier)." Comparisons to others can lead to very painful feelings when we aren't happy with our physical appearance or stamina. As we explored in the session on thoughts, as we think, so we become. When our internal dialogue is full of dislike and complaints about our bodies, we are actually building a body image that doesn't measure up to what it could potentially be.

> "I am whole, perfect, strong and powerful, loving, harmonious and peaceful."
> Audle Allison

Objectives:

Group members will:
* play with their body image as a way to improve it
* build a more positive relationship with their physical selves
* celebrate their positive physical qualities
* create an artistic model of their bodies

Materials:

Large paper: You will need enough so that each group member can lie down on his or her own sheet and have the outline of his or her body traced. Examples are: A roll of butcher paper, a large roll of newsprint, a roll of bulletin board paper in a neutral color, newsprint sheets, which could be taped together

Markers

Scissors

Glue: quick drying and clear

Miscellaneous art materials (i.e. feathers, glitter, ribbons, shiny paper, sparkles, crayons. The bigger the variety, the better the portraits.)

Note:

You might ask the group members ahead of time to bring fun art supplies for today. They could ask teachers, search around the house, or even find things in nature.

Procedure:

Have students initially work in pairs. One will lie down on a piece of butcher paper, which they cut approximately to their body length. The other partner will trace around his or her partner's body with a crayon. (Note: The drawn body will not be shaped exactly right. That is part of the fun.) Then they switch places. When each partner has a model of him- or herself drawn on butcher paper, the task is to decorate it to express him- or herself positively. "Who am I?" is the question. "How can I positively express myself and my body in art?" Obviously the more art supplies that are available, the more varied the projects will be.

When the artwork is done, ask the group members each to write three positive words that are self expressive on their portrait.

My body is _____, _____ and _____.

Before time runs out, have them put away supplies. In the clean space, ask each member to stand holding their self-portraits. It is tremendously fun to look around at the group and see the creations.

Discussion Questions:

1. What were you trying to capture in your artwork?
2. In what ways were you successful?
3. How can you feel more like the "you" of your art project?
4. Are there any thoughts you have that get in the way of feeling good about your body? If so, what could you say instead?

Special Note:

For the next session, ask each member to bring in uplifting stories, clean jokes, inspirational tales, music, etc., to share with the group. Their contributions are vital for the next group meeting.

Taking Care of Me

Practice your Self-Massage again. It might be fun to lead someone else in it too, perhaps a brother, sister or friend.

What are ways in which you could take care of your body? Some suggestions are:

_____ run around the block

_____ take a hot bath

_____ relax with quiet music or a good book

_____ eat a piece of fruit

_____ drink eight glasses of water a day

Check off those that you can do.

Now write your own suggestions.

*_____

*_____

*_____

*_____

Pick one of these ideas, and do it now.

Draw a Happy Face here when
you're done.

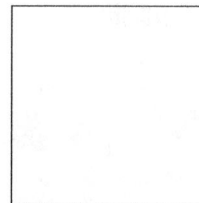

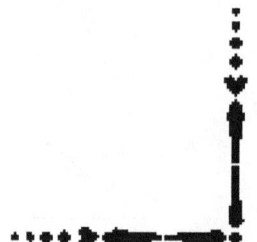

My Journal

Write a positive letter to your body.

Dear Body, Today I ... _____

_____

_____

_____

_____

_____

_____

_____

_____

Recall your group experience. Write about your thoughts, feelings and reactions.

_____

_____

_____

_____

_____

"I am whole, perfect, strong and powerful, loving, harmonious and peaceful."
Audle Allison

_____

The Healing Power of Compassion, Humor and Joy

These two sessions offer an interesting opportunity to explore three powerful components of healing: compassion, humor and joy. When we remember that the members of this group have come together because they are hurting in some way, it sheds light on the importance of these three aspects of healing.

First, kids who are hurting often feel powerless, vindictive and unloving. Their "love tanks," so to speak, may be empty or badly depleted. It may be next to impossible for them to step outside of themselves and their own hurt long enough to extend a compassionate hand to someone else. If they could, that very act of offering might open the door for compassion to flow back to them. Remember, we get what we give.

At best, kids who are hurting may be drawn to offer sympathy to their peers. Unfortunately, sympathy fosters dependence, as well as pulls kids right into the struggles that others are having. Think of a friend stuck in a mud puddle. Do we extend a rope from the safety of the edge, or jump in ourselves in a mistaken attempt to assist them? A good question to ask is: "Am I offering true support, or am I looking for an opportunity to thrill to the drama?" Sympathy gives the thrill.

Compassion, on the other hand, helps kids to bring about a change within themselves; it is empowering. It also breeds unconditional love, which is particularly vital when love tanks are already depleted. Although it may be difficult to cultivate compassion, one question that might inspire it is: "What good can come out of my sorrow and hurt?" The sought-for answers to this question can help to turn thinking from negative to positive, destructive to constructive.

Humor, the second powerhouse of this trio, is a wonderful key to opening up a saddened or hardened heart. We've all heard, "Laughter is the best medicine." Unfortunately, kids who are

> Step outside of your own pain by serving another.

hurting, especially because of a deep loss, often believe that it is inappropriate to laugh or play. They may need help to understand how laughter heals, as well as support in giving themselves permission to let go of the pain. They need to know that it is ok to Play! Play! Play! especially when feeling depressed or hurt. Make it a habit. Find a safe place to play (safe physically and emotionally). Make time and enjoy.

The final key in this trio is "joy." Joy can be born out of compassion and humor, but has a special flavor of its own. Joy has to do with holding an attitude of gratitude, of consciously looking for things to be grateful about, then holding those in our minds instead of focusing on the negative.

This is a lot of information to be taking in; I want you to know it is not your job in group to "teach" or "preach" these ideas. Instead, I encourage you to let them unfold through the activities. Look for signs of understanding, be supportive, offer insightful questions, and give inspiration. Be compassionate, humorous and joyful. In other words, be yourself.

> Make joyful play a habit.

The Feelings of Joy and Laughter

Prologue:

When I first tried this activity with kids, I was afraid they would resist it, or be unable to do it well. Was I wrong? They have frequently blown me away with their insightful contributions. Enjoy.

Objectives:

Group members will:
*   inspire and be inspired to feel joy and laughter
*   experience the importance of laughter in relationship to healing
*   develop compassion
*   experience the power of humor

Materials:

This session requires some pre-planning. At the end of last session, you gave directions for the group members to bring in uplifting stories, clean jokes, inspirational tales, music, etc. For this activity, the group members will come and sit in a circle with the things they brought with them.

Procedure:

Gather the group into a close circle so everyone can see everyone else's face. Invite members to share their stories, etc., one at a time. If it feels appropriate, you can elicit discussion along the way about why they chose the pieces they chose, or how those things impacted them, or the others. This can be a fruitful garden for spontaneous joy and discussion. I encourage you to share your examples, too.

Alternative Plan: Just in case, in the unlikely event that members do not come prepared, another plan would be to create your own version of an inspirational tale together. You can brainstorm ideas, write them on the board and create an original. I have done this with kids, too. It is fun and insightful.

> "Start every day off with a smile and get it over with."
> W.C. Fields

Discussion Questions:

1. What sorts of feelings did you experience during the story and joke telling?
2. What is it about laughter and joy that lightens our day?
3. Did any stories make you feel compassion? Sadness? Sympathy? Say more about that.
4. The comedian Will Rogers said: "Everything is funny as long as it is happening to someone else." What do you think this statement means?

Experience Sheet

Laughter Is Good Medicine

Get together with some friends or family and brainstorm as many funny and clean jokes as you can. Laugh ... Laugh ... Laugh ... (Did you know the library has joke books?)

Write you favorite joke here:

_____

_____

_____

_____

_____

_____

Ask some significant people in your life to tell you a story or tale from their lives that had meaning to them. You could ask parents, teachers, neighbors, the bus driver, etc. Lots of people have wonderful stories inside them just waiting to be told.

Write your favorite story here:

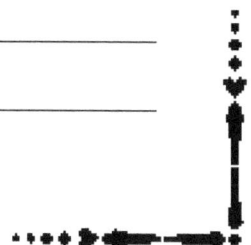

_____

_____

_____

_____

_____

_____

My Journal

Write about one of the funniest things that ever happened to you.

_____

_____

_____

_____

_____

_____

_____

_____

Recall your group experience. Write about your thoughts, feelings and reactions.

_____

_____

_____

_____

"Seven days without laughter makes one weak."
Mort Walker

_____

The Power of Gratitude

Prologue:

I started my first Gratitude Journal many years ago at the suggestion of a teacher who thought it might help me through some rocky times. I still love to go back and reread my early entries, and I continue to keep a Gratitude Journal to this day. It is a powerful way to focus on the positive. Also, by feeling grateful, I prime the pump for more abundance of all kinds to come my way.

Objectives:

Group members will:
* each create a Gratitude Journal in which they can record joyful memories
* start the process of thinking about things, events or people they are grateful for
* experience a joyful, creative time while making their books so they will have one shared memory to record

Materials:

The materials list depends on how simple or complicated you choose to make this process. One suggestion is to start with spiral notebooks that group members can decorate. By cutting and pasting from old magazines, they can create collages about themselves on their covers. In this case you need paste, magazines, scissors and notebooks.

If you have access to a binding machine, you can start with sheets of stock paper as covers, and use white or colored printer paper for the pages. This is fairly easy, and the members can decorate their covers with any type of art before binding.

Another simple idea is to use construction paper for the covers, and white printer paper for the inside sheets. If you use 8.5-by-11-inch sheets, you can fold them in half, along with the construction paper cover. Punch two holes near the center fold about 4 inches apart. Then tie string through the holes to hold the book together. Again, the covers can be decorated in any fashion.

Procedure:

You might say: "All of us have wonderful things in our worlds to be grateful for. Sometimes when the going gets tough, we may forget them. But they are there. For example, I am grateful for my body, which has a heart and lungs to keep me alive. I am grateful for my family, friends, and my pets, etc. (You can think about and share what is meaningful to you.)

"Today we are going to create a special place to record the things we are grateful for. It is called a Gratitude Journal. (If you have been keeping one of your own, you might bring it in to share at this point.) Because the things we are grateful for are special to us, we want our books to be special to us too, and to reflect who we are. I have brought with me materials to use to create our special books. They are ..."

And you are off and running. The main idea is to have fun while creating the books.

At the end, I suggest each member hold their own book, sit in a circle and have a moment to share it if they want to. Also, you could brainstorm some ideas to record, and maybe even provide a few moments to start writing. Often the hardest part of a Gratitude Journal is making the very first mark.

Discussion Questions:

1. What are some everyday events that you usually take for granted but that you might be grateful for? Why do you suppose you take them for granted?
2. Sometimes when we remember events to be grateful for, it is fun to say thank you to people involved. Can you think of any events for your Gratitude Journal that involve the opportunity to say "Thank you"?
3. What might be some good places to keep your Gratitude Journals to help develop a habit of remembering to write in them on a regular basis?

Never waste an opportunity to tell someone you love them.

H. Jackson Brown, Jr

Acts of Kindness

Think of four kind acts that people have done to or for you and write them here.

1. _____

_____

2. _____

_____

3. _____

_____

4. _____

_____

Now pick one and write the person a thank-you letter, expressing your gratitude for their kindness.

When your letter is done,
draw a Happy Face here:

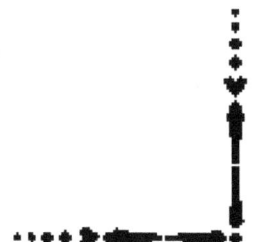

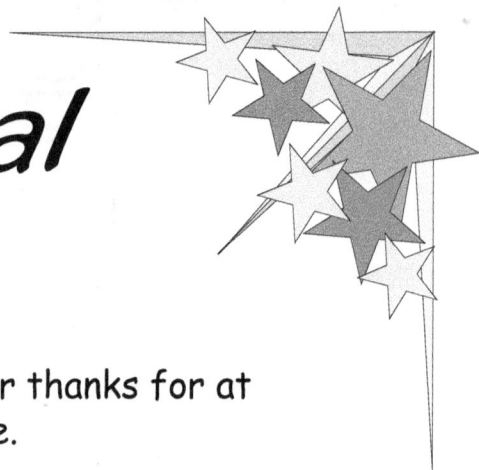

My Journal

Write a letter to yourself. In it, express your thanks for at least seven things about yourself that you like.

Dear Wonderful _____

(write your name)

_____

_____

_____

_____

_____

_____

_____

_____

_____

Recall your group experience. Write about your thoughts, feelings and reactions.

_____

_____

_____

_____

"It is amazing what you can accomplish if you do not care who gets the credit."

Harry S. Truman

_____

Recovery From Grief and Loss

This is a huge and sensitive area, and in the scope of this book, we can only touch on it. Kids who are really tender and torn may need further professional help.

I do believe that kids who are hurting from grief and loss can still receive and give support in a group of other kids who are working with their own individual types of hurt. In fact, their inclusion in the group can be a very powerful assistance to them as well as to others. As you approach this topic, remember these kids have been in group and sharing all along.

Although the two activities, "Healing a Broken Heart" and "Reflecting on Cherished Memories," are designed with grief and loss in mind, they are also suitable for all kids. Each of us has experienced our own losses. Some of us may have lost friends or relatives, others a beloved pet or cherished dream. In any case, these activities will be helpful in honoring the pain and letting it go.

I release and
let go.

Healing a Broken Heart

Prologue:

I've done this activity with kids and adults, and it never ceases to amaze me how healing it is to visually depict a broken heart, then graphically see it healed. It provides both empowerment and hope.

Objectives:

Group members will:
* explore what makes a heart feel broken
* explore supportive ways to heal a broken heart
* select something they can do to support themselves or another
* offer support to others in the hurting/healing process

Materials:

Poster board or chart paper with a large heart draw on it,
   jaggedly cut in half to depict a broken heart.
One paper heart about 6 inches tall for each group member
One paper heart about 8 inches tall for each group member
Pens, pencils or markers
Glue or tape

Procedure:

Introduce the activity by displaying the poster board with the large "broken" heart. Ask members what impressions they have when they look at the large broken heart. What feelings does it trigger for them? Is there anything they want to share about their own hearts? Their own hurts?

After the discussion, pass out the 6-inch hearts, one per person. Instruct the group members to tear the hearts in half, then write words or draw simple pictures on each half that are suggestive of a broken heart. Perhaps it is a way they feel, or have felt. Or it might be a few words to describe a specific incident that caused hurt.

Cover the large poster board-broken heart with the smaller torn ones by pasting them on, providing an opportunity for members to share briefly if they choose to as they paste up their broken hearts.

Next, invite the group to briefly discuss ideas they think might be helpful to heal the broken heart. Pass out the 8-inch hearts, one per person. With their paper hearts intact, ask members to write or draw what it might take for the broken heart to heal or feel more whole.

Now cover the large poster board-heart with these healing suggestions, while providing members an opportunity to share briefly as they hang their 8-inch hearts.

Discussion Questions:

1. What observations do you notice about the covered heart?
2. In what way(s) might it resemble or not resemble your own heart?
3. What might be one suggestion that you heard today that you can put to use in your own life?
4. How might you offer support to someone else who is hurting?

Special Note:

If time allows at the end of this session, it would be a great time to review the Self-Massage activity.

Healing A Hurt

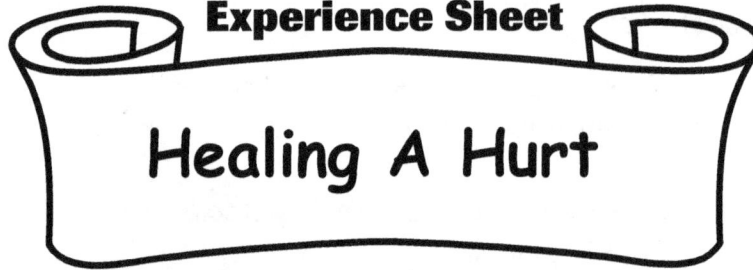

One of the best ways to heal a hurting heart is to be kind to yourself and others. Do you know anyone who could use your kindness? In what ways could you show it? Write or draw your ideas here.

Sometimes when you feel sad about someone or something that dies, you may have thoughts and feelings you didn't get an opportunity to share. It often helps to express those thoughts and feelings by drawing a picture. After it is done, you can even tear it up as a way to let go. The idea is to get your feelings out. Think about someone or something you've had to let go of, perhaps through a death. Draw a picture to express your thoughts and feelings.

When your artwork is done, write how you feel as a result of drawing the picture.

_____

_____

My Journal

Write a "thank you" letter to a person, animal or thing you have had to let go of. In it, express your gratitude for how your life was touched in a positive way.

_____

_____

_____

_____

_____

_____

_____

_____

_____

Recall your group experience. Write about your thoughts, feelings and reactions.

_____

_____

_____

_____

_____

"Keep your face to the sunshine and you cannot see the shadow."
Helen Keller

_____

Reflecting On Cherished Memories

Prologue:

There is something almost tangible about the written word in poetry form. Memory Poems serve a beautiful function as they give form to cherished memories, and create an opportunity to share in a safe and structured way.

Objectives:

Group members will:
* recall poignant memories
* reflect and write about the memories
* share poetry and memories
* discuss the process of releasing memories

Materials:

Paper
Pens or Pencils
Experience Sheets for each group member

Procedure:

Start the activity by asking group members to reflect on things and/or people in their past (far or recent) that they treasure. Suggest the memory could be about something tangible or not, but something or someone who has impacted them in a real way. If might be helpful to brainstorm and jot down a list of ideas to get the process started.

Introduce the structure of The Memory Poem, and read examples, noting how the examples fit the format.

Take just a few moments to write a poem as a group about something the members have in common (i.e. school food or a loved mascot).

Once they get the idea, have them individually reflect and write their own Memory Poems. Encourage helpful, supportive talk and sharing.

"When we recall the past, we usually find that it is the simplest things, not the great occasions, that in retrospect give off the greatest glow of happiness."
Bob Hope

Near the end of the session, invite group members to share poems aloud if they choose, with time to discuss why they chose to write about that topic. Remember, all poems are special.

Memory Poem Structure

One: One word naming memory
Two: Four words that describe it
Three: Where was the memory created
Four: Why you like this thing or person
Five: Special times you shared together
Six: What happened to the person or thing
Seven: Feeling you have about thing/person

Person Example

Free
Foster, Joyous, Chubby, Sweet
Lived with me on Delaware Street
Always gave me baby kisses
Eating sand on California coast
Moved back with own family
Love forever

Thing Example

Ice skates
White, sharp, shining, fast
On frozen ponds in Michigan
Gift from favorite grandpa
Skated with friends and shared hot chocolate
Gave to younger cousin
Joy

Discussion Questions:

1. In what way do we own our memories, or they own us?
2. What part of remembering is positive? Negative?
3. If we have hurtful memories, what are some ways to let them go?
4. How do we remember and keep our happy memories?

Memory Poem

_____
(One word recalling your memory)

_____ , _____ , _____ and _____
(Four words that describe your memory)

_____
(Where was the memory created?)

_____
(Why did you like this thing or person?)

_____
(Special times you shared together)

_____
(What happened to the person or thing?)

_____
(Feeling you have about this person or thing)

1. Find a friend or family member to write a person and/or thing Memory Poem with. You could teach them the pattern, and enjoy sharing ideas and time.

2. Do you know anyone who is experiencing a painful time now? In what way could you reach out to that person to be kind and caring? For example, could you make a card, call him or her up, or give a surprise hug? Write your idea here: _____

_____

Make a Happy Face when you
have been kind to someone.

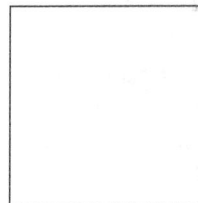

My Journal

Write about or draw a picture of a special memory.

Recall your group experience. Write about your thoughts, feelings and reactions.

_____

_____

_____

_____

_____

"Very little is needed to make a happy life. It is all within yourself, in your way of thinking."

Marcus Aurelius

_____

Goal Setting and Service to Others

A theme I have emphasized throughout this book is that by our thinking we really do create our immediate realities. We don't have to be victims to our negative thinking. Instead, we can decide how we want our lives to be, and head in that direction, even if we can only do it initially in our minds.

How do we do that? We set goals. Instead of dwelling too long on the misery, the sadness, the abuse, or whatever is stealing our joy, we can refocus our thinking to develop a way out of sadness and into joy. Remember, it is appropriate to grieve, and it is also proper to let go and move on.

When beginning a goal-setting session, some excellent questions to ask yourself are: Who do I want to be? How do I want my life to be? How do I want to feel? Think? Believe?

Another theme throughout this book has to do with service and the power of healing that comes from giving to and caring for others. The activities included in this section on "Goal Setting and Service to Others" capitalize on this theme. As a group, members will be learning a goal-setting process, creating a plan, carrying out a service project, and exploring how it feels to give of themselves. In a way, they are taking all of their experience from the past weeks in group and putting it to work.

"Act and ye shall succeed."
Susanna Palomares

This section is designed to be completed in two sessions; you may choose to expand the time by creating an extended service project if that is appropriate for you and your group. I do, however, want to emphasize that "Goal Setting and Service to Others" can be very powerful without being complicated. By following the model and serving others, the objectives of this section will be met.

Moving Forward with Goal Setting

Prologue:

How do we program for what we want? We set goals. Through setting and achieving goals, we have an opportunity to feel power, movement and energy in motion. We can begin to move out of the sadness and hurt into a future of joy. Of course, there will be other hurts along the way, but life does not have to be dominated by the pain.

Objectives:

Group members will:
* explore what makes a goal
* practice the steps of goal setting
* plan a service project

Materials:

A "Service Project Planning Form" for each participant
Chart pad
Markers

Procedure:

You might say: "In this group session and the next one, we will be creating and doing a project that will not only be enjoyable for us, but can be of service to someone else. In order to carry out our project, we'll look at a model for goal setting, decide what we want to do, make a plan, then do it. The model is written on the "Service Project Planning Form", so let's explore it together."

At this point, give everyone a copy of the "Service Project Planning Form" and read it together to get a general overview. Then go back to the beginning and, as a group, work through the plan step-by-step recording all necessary information on the chart pad.

> If I don't do my own thinking, something else will fill my brain.

Step 1:

Identify a problem or need within the school or the community at large. Together, brainstorm and record a list of ideas onto the chart pad. For example:

Need or Problem

trash on school grounds
graffiti
hospitalized children
seniors in a center
beautify a park

(It would be helpful to know ahead of time if the possibility exists to leave the school grounds, and if any funds are available.)

Step 2:

Think about what could be done to resolve or help reduce each of the brainstormed needs or problems. For example:

NEED	SERVICE
trash on school grounds	pick up trash
graffiti	paint over the graffiti
hospitalized children	make and send cards
seniors in a center	visit a senior center
beautify a park	plant a tree or flower bed

Give joy,
feel joyful.

Step 3:

Encourage discussion of the pros and cons and feasibility of each service possibility and then, as a group, pick one of the options. (Given time and proximity constraints, I encourage simplicity. As I mentioned earlier, this session can be very powerful without being complicated.)

Step 4:

On a clean sheet of chart paper write the chosen service project in the form of a goal. Make sure the goal meets these three criteria: it is achievable, measurable and time limited. For example: Within two weeks we will paint over the graffiti on the south wall of our school.

Step 5:

Each member signs the goal statement on the chart pad to demonstrate support and agreement.

Step 6:

Generate the plan. This step involves discussion, give and take, brainstorming and good positive energy. When the plan is complete, everyone will know specifically what needs to be done, by whom, when, about permission slips if needed, what supplies and/or money are necessary, etc. It is important that each group member have a part, and know clearly what that part is.

Step 7:

Choose a way to acknowledge the completion of the project. It is through this acknowledgment that success can be measured and celebrated.

"My greatest joy is to serve."
Audie Allison

Discussion Questions:

1. What qualities did group members display that helped the group to be successful today?
2. If there were any things that got in the way of success, what were they? How could you have improved in those areas?
3. What feelings were being experienced during today's process? And what thoughts might have led to those feelings?
4. How are you feeling about doing the project?
5. How do we help ourselves by helping others?

Service Project Planning Form

1. Identify a problem or need.

2. What could be done with each of the problems or needs?

3. After discussion and deliberation, decide on one of the options.

4. Set a goal that meets these three criteria:
    a. It must be achievable; in other words, you really can do it.
    b. It must be measurable. You should be able to prove or show you did it.
    c. It must have a time limit, so you know when it is complete.

5. Every member signs the goal to demonstrate agreement.

6. Create a plan. Be sure to answer the following questions:
    a. What are all the tasks that need to be done in order to achieve this specific goal?
    b. Who will do what? (Assign people to individual tasks.)
    c. When will each task be done?
    d. What permissions are needed?
    e. If money is needed, how much and from where?
    f. What supplies are needed?

7. Decide how you will acknowledge your success and the completion of your service project.

List your personal responsibilities, what you will have to do, in order for this group service project to be a success.

_____

_____

_____

_____

Experiencing Kindness and Service to Others

Prologue:

Today participants will experience the benefits of kindness, service and extending a compassionate hand to others as they fulfill the goals of the service project they established. The group will have an opportunity to take their collective energy and direct it in a way that moves the focus from themselves to others. This is a heartwarming day, fueled by positive action, which can move members out of pain and into healing.

Objectives:

Group members will:
* implement a goal-setting model
* perform a service project
* explore the personal benefits of performing acts of service to others

Materials:

A list of materials can be generated once the specific service project has been planned.

Procedure:

The specifics of this day will depend entirely on what goal was set last session, and what plans were made by the group to implement the goal. It is important to have fun and enjoy the process of performing the service project. This will be the final session the group will spend together, except for closure. Let it count.

At the end of the project, spend some time debriefing by discussing the results, congratulating yourselves on the success, and considering what it feels like to help others. Remember to acknowledge the results in the agreed-upon way. Finally, today's Experience Sheet will provide paricipants a place to reflect on what they have learned about goal setting from the service project and to apply these learnings to their own lives. By recording some persoanl goals, they are visualizing their lives moving beyond pain and loss into a bright future.

Discussion Questions:

1. In what ways did the planning help you to be successful in your service project?
2. What are some areas you could have improved on? How?
3. How did you benefit from your service to others?
4. In what ways can you individually use the knowledge from this session outside of the group?
5. Did you notice any actions or reactions from others in response to the service project you performed? If so, what?

Goal Setting and Achieving

A goal is something you work for, move toward, and finally reach. When you have goals, you know exactly where you're going and what you have to do to get there. It's kind of like having a road map to guide you to your destination. And when you put your goals in writing, you are more likely to achieve them. Written goals can be reviewed regularly and have more power. Like a contract with yourself, they are harder to neglect or forget.

When John Goddard was 15 years old, he wrote a list of 127 goals he wanted to achieve in his lifetime. His list included things like climbing Mt. Everest, exploring the Nile River, running a five-minute mile, writing a book, and learning to play the piano. He went on to become a world famous explorer and adventurer and by the time he was 65, he had accomplished 105 of his 127 goals. He has lived a very exciting life that was shaped by the goals he set when he was 15.

What kind of goals are you setting for yourself? Dream about some of the things you would like to do in your lifetime and list them below.

Here are 10 BIG things I want to do in my life:

1. _____   6. _____

2. _____   7. _____

3. _____   8. _____

4. _____   9. _____

5. _____   10. _____

My Journal

How do you feel when you do something that helps others?

_____

_____

_____

_____

_____

_____

_____

_____

_____

_____

Recall your group experience. Write about your thoughts, feelings and reactions.

_____

_____

_____

_____

_____

"It's kind of fun to do the impossible."
Walt Disney

Section III

This last section provides lesson plans only for the last day of the group. It offers activities for final group reflection, evaluation, celebration and saying goodbye. Even if some of the activities in Section II are eliminated, positive closure in a group setting is critical. I suggest these activities, like those in Section I, be done by each group.

Closure

Prologue:

The final day of the group and sometimes the last day or two leading up to closure, can be traumatic times for kids who have not only bonded to the leader, but also to each other. This is especially true in a group for kids who hurt. They come to the group feeling vulnerable, thus they often highly value the support and friendships that have developed throughout the weeks. Letting go of the group is, in fact, a form of loss.

There are many common reactions to closures. Some kids may deny the end and walk out saying: "See ya next week." Others may withdraw or even become uncooperative: "I don't like this stupid group anyway." Others may express sadness by crying, hugging and acting clingy. Whatever the response, each group member will deal with the closure in his or her own way.

As a leader, you will also experience your own form of closure. Often I feel a mixture of joy and sorrow; it's not at all unusual for me to cry when saying goodbye. This is a particularly good time to keep the tissue box close by.

The other side of closure is the celebration at having accomplished goals, completed projects, taken many risks, and formulated new ways of being. I think it is particularly important to do some form of activity to consciously recognize the ending, perhaps a ritual that all participate in to say goodbye.

It is also important to gather feedback. This not only serves you, the leader, for planning future groups, but gives the participants a voice and opportunity to finish unspoken business. I think it is vital.

As in the first day, this last day has several activities that make up the session. Each part adds a special dimension to the process of closure and saying goodbye.

Part 1
Feedback

Objectives:

Group members will:
*   provide feedback about their experience in the group
*   complete a written evaluation form

Materials:

One Group Evaluation Form per participant
Pen or pencil for each participant

Procedure:

You might say: "As we are reaching the end of our sessions together, I want you to know how much I value and appreciate your ideas and feelings. In order to make these group sessions better and better for others, please take a few minutes to fill out the Group Evaluation Form. Be sure to notice that your name is optional."

Pass out the forms with pens or pencils and allow time for writing. Then collect the forms to review at a later date. Ask the participants if they have any comments they would like to share.

Part 2
Getting Closure

Objectives:

Group members will:
*   have a chance to say goodbye verbally
*   experience a safe space for feelings generated by closure
*   celebrate successes experienced in the group

Materials:

A special object that can be held by each member in turn. (Examples: A pink rose or a heart are two items that have meaning from previous sessions. Other options might be a pretty stone, a candle, a seashell, a piece of art, etc.)

Procedure:

Have the whole group stand in a circle.

One member takes the object in his or her hands. While holding it, he or she addresses the subject: "The significance of this group to me has been ..." When done speaking, he or she passes the object to the next person, who addresses the same subject.

When all of the members, including the leader(s) have spoken, the last speaker holds the object into the center of the circle with his or her right hand. All the other group members then reach out with right hands to simultaneously touch the hand in the center, so all hands touch.

As the leader, you then might say: "Look around the circle at the eyes of each group member. See how collectively we are special, and individually we are special too. As you leave today, take with you the memory of this group, and let it hold you up in times of trouble, and celebrate with you in times of joy."

Then ask the group to slowly back away from each other, softly repeating the words: Joy Joy Joy Joy Joy Joy Joy

Part 3
Celebration and Good-bye

Objectives:

Group members will:
* Laugh and have fun
* Celebrate with food.

Materials:

A few simple refreshments, something festive and celebratory.

Procedure:

Eat and be merry. Allow time at the end of the session for cleanup and hugs. Even encourage each member to hug him- or herself.

See that each person gets a final Experience Sheet and Journal page before going out the door.

I encourage you to be fully present for goodbyes. Enjoy the final eye contact, final smiles and final hugs. Seize the moment. And give yourself a big hug too. You deserve it.

"Finally, in conclusion, let me say just this."
Peter Sellers

Group Evaluation Form

Name (optional) _____ Date _____

1. What was it about this group that you liked?

2. What was most helpful to you?

3. What was hard for you, but still worth doing?

4. Would you recommend this group? Why or why not?

5. Any other ideas or suggestions?

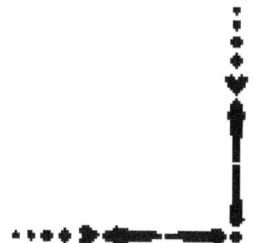

Experience Sheet

Self Reflection

Reflect and write about the following:

Something I learned from being in this group is:

_____

_____

_____

_____

_____

I was able to contribute to the group in the following ways:

_____

_____

_____

_____

Remember that part of what makes us feel joyful is being kind and gentle to others. Can you think of ways to continue those behaviors now that the group is over? Write a list or draw pictures below to help you remember.

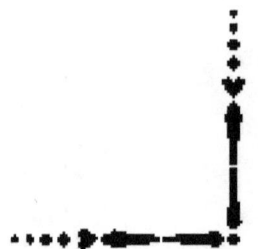

My Journal

Jot down the names of each group member. Next to each name, write something about that person that you are grateful for. Be sure to include yourself.

_____

_____

_____

_____

_____

_____

_____

_____

_____

Recall your group experience. Write about your thoughts, feelings and reactions.

_____

_____

_____

_____

"A friend is a present you give yourself."
Robert Louis Stevenson

_____

If your heart is in Social-Emotional
Learning, visit us online.

Come see us at
www.InnerchoicePublishing.com

Our web site gives you a look at all our other Social-Emotional
Learning-based books, free activities, articles, research, and
learning and teaching strategies. Every week you'll get a new
Sharing Circle topic and lesson.

INNERCHOICE Publishing
15079 Oak Chase Court
Wellington, FL 33414

* 9 7 8 1 5 6 4 9 9 0 7 7 8 *